Notes from Refuge

poems by

Lana Maht Wiggins

Plain View Press
P. O. 42255
Austin, TX 78704

plainviewpress.net
sb@plainviewpress.net
1-512-441-2452

Copyright Lana Maht Wiggins, 2008. All rights reserved.
ISBN: 978-1-891386-34-3
Library of Congress Number: 2008926911

Cover Art: "New Hope Stairs" © John Fink, Jr.
www.finksterproductions.com

Special thanks to Richard Turek of Heavenly Creatures for the French translation of "E. Bathory's Prayer."

For my mother,
Marie

Acknowledgments

The following poems have appeared in *The Southwestern Review*: "Breaking Down Divorce," "A Fragment of Chaos Suspended from the Whole," "Driving West," and "Reflection of Fear." "Human Conditions" appeared in *Knock* 3.2, Fall 2006. "Signature Hamartia" appeared in *Moondance* Exploration Issue, 2006.

"Three Photographs, Three Days" appeared in *Dance to Death*, Issue II, 2006. "Cracker Jack Voodoo," Refuge Chaos," and "Nagasaki Butterfly" have appeared in *Words-Myth* Issue # 4, 2006."E. Bathory's Prayer," "Teacups and Tin Men," "Grace Note Two," and "Ode to H.D." have appeared in *The Smoking Poet* Issue 4, Fall 2007.

The University of Louisiana at Lafayette originally published the following poems in 2001 in a Master of Art thesis titled *First Person, Twice Removed: Poetic Conversations in an Evolving Woman's Voice*: "O Shit," "Single Morning," "Nagasaki Butterfly," "Ode to H.D.," "Surviving Identity," "Losing My Balance While Rising," "Reflection of Fear," "A Fragment of Chaos Suspended From the Whole," "Tattoo," "Driving West," "My Sister Sees Signs In Everything," "The Wreck Revisited," "Kitchen Poetics," "Grace Note One" and "Things Mina Loy Couldn't Say."

Special thanks to the Creative Writing Department of the University of Louisiana, Lafayette, especially Jerry McGuire, Darrell Bourque, and Skip Fox for their support over the years, the University of New Orleans for taking a chance on me, Luis Urrea for showing me how wide my wings, Theresa Wiggins for lending me her poetry and inspiration, Tom and Tommy Wiggins for their voices of reason, Cheryl Estrada for always speaking in poetry and reading the signs, Rhonda Robison for sharpening her analytic knife on my words so gracefully, Keith Roy for showing me beauty in life and death, and especially Jacques Sirgent for showing me there is beauty in life after death and for believing in my words and thoughts – you are my heart, my life, my teacher, my poet, my salvation. Without you, this book would not be.

Contents

I.
New Orleans Blue from the Eye and I of the Storm   7

Cracker Jack Voodoo   9
Human Conditions   11
Bending Meaning   13
O Shit   14
My Sister Sees Signs In Everything   16
Driving West   17
Nine Days Before The Storm   18
Evidence of Existence   22
Refuge Chaos   24
Notes From Refuge   25
Detour Of Destiny   26
Tempting Fate   27
Single Morning   28
Signature Hamartia   29

II.
Suicide and Grace Notes   31
E. Bathory's Prayer   33
Prière d'E. Báthory   35
Suicide Notes   37
Losing My Balance While Rising   38
Bipolar Rage   39
Alter: ego   40
Breaking Down Divorce   42
Event Horizon   43
Ode To H.D.   44
Grace Note One   45
Blue Skies   46
Maja's Seduction   47
Your Hands   48
Grace Note Two   49
I Want   50
Moon Stroke   51
Tattoo   52
The Wreck Revisited   53
Things Mina Loy Couldn't Say   54

Nagasaki Butterfly   56

III.
Fragments of Chaos Suspended From the Whole   57

The Other Side   59
Kitchen Poetics   60
Lousiana Garden In August   62
Precipice Of a Third Story Edge 63
A Fragment Of Chaos Suspended From The Whole   65
Surviving Identity   66
Three Photographs, Three Days 67
Reflection Of Fear   69
Near-Drowning   71
Teacups and Tin Men   72
Earth/Air   73
Primal   74
Theresa's Rant   75
Voodoo Moss   78
End Note 80

About the Author   81

I.

New Orleans Blue from the Eye and I of the Storm

Cracker Jack Voodoo

In my mother's New Orleans
of Buster Brown Bodegas
and nectar-soda café stools,
a Canal St. Saturday was a ticket to the good life.

Strolling the boulevard in pin-up pumps,
watching Cabrini-girls flip
ponytails and church-made skirts,
she slips into McCrory's five and dime
for a heart-shaped bottle and a block of paraffin.
Her next stop is Woolworth's for a sweet and 5 cent soda.

The Rampart corner is hopping-slick.
Zootsuit hawkers tappin' and callin'
fine ladies and gents sifting tailor-made bargains.
Bugle-boys strutting Stacy Adams spats,
and finely woven fedoras they'll hock later to make rent.

Mama goes to Rampart for Cracker Jack Voodoo.
A chicken foot and some *gris-gris* oils.
One to keep evil out Sunday morning,
the other to keep it in Saturday night.
Old men calculate her formula in a red *grimoire*.

My mother bundles magic in a straw bag,
hops an Uptown streetcar
to shop windows beside Creole beauties
in pink-dot peplums and black pinwheels,
kid-glove fingers,
and twenty-dollar handbags.

In my New Orleans
of Gutter Girl Galleries
and hand-grenade street puke,
a Canal Saturday is freak surreality.

In black boot comfort,
I watch Cabrini-girls trip
in Manolo heels over purple beads,
and NOPD horse-shit at Razzoo.
Foamy frat boys grabbin' and howlin',
strutting Abercrombie and Phat Farm.
Bugle-boys struggling to pull in a dollar
for A&P's 32 special.
Creole beauties shoplift iPods
from broken windows, and 5 cents
in your pocket
buys a sweet ticket to jail.

I get my Voodoo in Jackson Square.
A chicken foot and some *gris-gris* oils.

The Square corner is a Cracker Jack knock-off.
Rampart is a parking lot now.

Since commiserating company is somewhat under-rated,
we take our loan from the graces,
my mother and I.
She with lace covered hair,
kneeling solemnly on a *prie-dieu*,
posturing piety for laconic virgins shrouded.

I feign bravado with black shawl shoulders
in throes of plaintive tribulation.

Despite our differences,
cloaked in esoteric sublime,
my body is my mother's.

Human Conditions

Filip: "Laruskha, Larushka, oh my beloved Larushka"
Sasha: "You are a small animal chewing its fur. Stop talking."
Filip: "Cook some meat."

So much lost in translation,
my Russian comrades draw blank
on chocolate city discussions and T-shirts,
reconstructing a broke-down city
edging something like a condition.

Today, I am a small girl in mother's clothes.
Too-big shoes stuffed with yellow tissue,
a blouse twice the size of my accomplishments.
Times like these I want the charade of my charade to halt.

Who am I to pretend that I am
more than a river's reflection flooding
conscious streams?
I am an intruder in my own life and home,
out of place, time, fashion, luck –
a vampire in blue jeans and sunlight.

What is lost in translation is found
in propaganda of respective history lessons.
As children, the comrades played German soldiers
13 kilometers from Moscow,
facing Stalingrad's offensive in starched uniform
against Belarusians clinging to 3 percent lives.
American boys memorized Normandy heroics, Native annihilation –
each convinced we were the world's salvation.

We share common sufferings –
fathers spending lifetimes awakening something that was never in us.

So we cling to post-Cold War camaraderie today,
wonder at the capacity for cruelty in politiomaniacal greed
of mustached and bearded *upyr* ancestors lining our mantles.

To forget who we were, we toast another shot of Absolut,
sit back – explain Russian ketchup, American hotdogs.

Bending Meaning

He argued that *mentis orgasma* was incorrect Latin
when all I wanted was to point out the obvious.
But he was too into being in two
stimuli modes of gadget intelligence and self-importance.

Just once, I say, embrace flexibility,
hold it like an exotic new lover in spiked red heels.

Question the grand illusion of being
correct in everything.
Think of the infinite possibilities of dust.

Just once, I say, walk through a crowded room
with disbelief of everything you know suspending.
Collect vibrations of someone else for a change,
and explore poetic bends of meaning.

O Shit

one more time and i think i'll get it right
   the damn melody keeps playing in my head
but the rhythm slips away at the chorus

tonight i'm gonna own this
fucking agony
and tomorrow i'll look
for the first morning fugue
and if the rays on the wall remind me
i'll swing my legs over the bed
brush my hair
and

i will not write about
   slow saxophones or you
   at the piano or the vein
   of music that makes you
   tap my arm in your sleep

i will not write about
   half-step interludes of grace
   notes poised so fragile
   or dissonant arpeggios in 12-
   bar blues call and response

if i can stop myself
from writing this poem
it will fade into something
like overtures you might hear in an elevator
or this dunghill of words i'll throw
away tonight because i must work
on this rhythm
   one more time and i think i'll get it right

if it slips away again
and i cannot turn the phrase
then i will not comfort myself
with a cold blade at my wrist
or a bandage of inadequate language
i will not write this poem

My Sister Sees Signs In Everything

for Cheryl

We cling to tender omens
Our greatest secret in the smallest part
   Of our bodies
With you, I do not remember
The law of paradigms
Only rituals of early morning wishes
   Jazz-blue summers
Spooning ice cream into iridescent mouths
Finding sky or home
Under the circle of trees

We search for signs
In familiar strangers
Each one a mirror of you
I, the coward in lighthouse shadow
Growing less and less weary of the finite

We rush legitimacy
Knowing the crime
To bury a ring of angels
Even then you see the signs
And travel the distance of compromise

We open to metamorphosis
Become warrior in celestial mask
Splinter in the geography of horizon
And hover skyline tower
   At sunrise

We pick at portals of damnation
Seek simile and metaphor in curse
   And lie   at midnight
Face up   in the backyard garden

Driving West

At 7:25, colors merge
into blurred shapes of grey
rice fields in Crowley, Louisiana.
Morning is a matted illusion.

I'm driving West today.

Stretching this dusty backroad
with a gilded mirror for company
and all expectations behind me.

I'll be a dark-eyed shimmer of paradise.
Scheherazade or Pandora
in a wheat-berry desert.

A girl raised on southern sun
cuts like a razor on your back.

I've felt the shameless seduction
of oil-black mud
bleeding around my ankles.

Drifted the soil of my body
in gumbo rivers
that lick a fever clean.

I am a woman,
wet, wild, warm, and worn.

Nine Days Before The Storm

Five parking tickets and a summer in Big Easy,
now you know the blues, money, and Jelly's roll through Storyville.
Today is a sunflower slow drag with Satchmo, Jesus, and Merlin,
howling at the moon on a tarot-read square 'cause
the Easy is tough for a girl painting apples and rainbows on a dime.

Forty-one Frenchmen and you can't read these notes.
Shit, nobody can decipher the madmen walking this city.
You'll find Magic and Voodoo on Rampart and Dumaine,
teachers or priests in pentagram chaos across the river.
If you look real hard you might find Norma Wallace
under your bed with Big Jim or some other Vidalia.

You want to go home, but there ain't no place like it
with all these bloody secrets behind nailed shut windows,
and two-bit hustlers lining the streets like day-lilies after rain.
Tourists on every corner with shopping bags and flip-flops,
bead hustling hags, and 3rd floor ghosts on display.

If you ain't blue after walking the Quarter all night,
then you got no soul and you're just a tin can drum.
If you want to see how easy the Easy is,
ferry over to Algiers to watch the Cathedral fade
with a half moon river of unwashed bodies,
then synchronize too many years of history in just one night.

The hardest thing you'll ever do is leave everything you know
to love this strange land with strangers and strangelings
distorting language so you hate the sound of "r"
now as it rolls from your tongue,
and everything in the Market scares you
because only the pigeons know your face.

New Orleans is a Bourbon-blue-Royal-blend nightmare
to someone hiding behind an iron fence of empathy,
feeling every body's thoughts and hearing every body's pain,
because dealing with your own is more than a girl can handle
on a stormy night in this new Gotham city dyed black and undead.

You're eating shit out of a can and flipping coins all day,
waiting for your life to begin sometime next year.
If you spread a little sea salt and rub a small crystal,
you might work some magic for tomorrow.
But the trouble begins when you try to reconcile your gods
with Liberty and Justice for all.

But isn't this the way it always is when you're on a verge?

Squeaky and that Russian son-of-a-cat are trying to breathe your air,
but you're learning selfishness from scratch.
Counting day one everyday until you somehow get to day two
and manage to live without hope in a bottle or a bag
of something these people can't steal on St. Louie's steps.

St. Germain wants you to be eyes and ears
at the Ursulines and Royal corner,
but you ain't got 2.5 cents much less million,
so these saints will have to wait or cough up some dough
for Miss Janey and you to write down these memories.

Poems aren't free and they sure don't come easy
when you got nothing but dirt under your nails,
and ghosts slip beneath your covers to orchestrate
another dream sequence that makes perfect nonsense,
except to dragons and other winged things patrolling the astral.

Because nothing's real in New Orleans,
except the sound of your mama's voice ringing in your ears
and the growl of your belly against the floor.

But you can't leave until you find yourself
floating on the Mississippi, and know you are who they said
you are back home with all those awards
papered on the walls in red ink.

Knowing the outcome ahead of time is suicide for the soul.
Still you maintain dignity under nihilistic bouts of depression
that sets you apart from the usual crowd of misfits
posing as artists or soothsaying mysterians with a deck of cards
and a five dollar table covered in raw stones.

You don't know why you love her too much to notice
those bloody cracks on the edge of her crescent,
surviving under the sea-level rise of steamboat polluted air,
and the uptown politicos in grey suits and polished skin,
making groceries and the rent every month on time.

You're never disappointed in the man who asks for a dollar every
time you pass his post on St. Ann, because he nods politely
when you pat your empty handed pockets.
Because he knows what it feels like to want
something you can't have and to have something you can't want.

Every day you announce your arrival in New Orleans
with a loud shout and a shit-eating grin.
Handing out copies of a worthless degree
and a packet of poems nobody reads or feels.
Because nothing matters here except who your daddy knows.
So the man behind the Western Union glass knows more about you
than anybody here and he ain't worried 'cause he gets his 2 %
whether you eat or not tonight is your own business.

Finally the day comes when they call you back,
but there are 25 other girls in shorter skirts and smoother hair,
so you suck it up as you pack it up,
making that long walk to Esplanade in high heels,

stumbling on broken sidewalks,
thinking any day could be *the* day
Dixies start to roll in and you can
finally get that boot off your car.

You're too scared to hope because the blues got you good.
So you go out and dance in the street for a dollar and smile
while you pick white wisteria and catch another second line.
Then crawl home Scarlett O'Hara style
with a pocket of dust
and Draconian dreams of tomorrow as just one more day.

(8/20/2005)

Evidence of Existence

Your first thoughts are about what you will save.
Then the long drive west again to refuge.

Revelations of self-induced illusions,
dreams of poetic license,
accomplishments all become trivial –
A son, a daughter, and 3 cats are everything
you cannot bear to lose in a Category 4.

There is no easy way to prepare for this storm.
You sandbag and board,
knowing the futility.
God himself will not stop this truculent water dragon
bearing down upon ancient and agnostic levees
of the New Atlantis soup bowl with such malevolent grace.

You are Noah fleeing an unsound Ark.
Thoth carving the final hieroglyphs
on rancid streets of callous nefarium.
You are certain you will survive.

Forty days later, you reach down
to pull yourself up by the boot straps,
but the boots are gone too.

There is nothing but memories of things.
One hopeful mystic on Cathedral steps,
cryptic body-count symbols on every standing structure . . .

No stages, no audience, no one to impress
with eons of music and history
or paranormal activity of gothic apparitions.

All that remain are gruesome reflections of toxic water
receding and revealing hybrid mold,
a thousand neophyte ghosts,
nine wards of annihilation,
and pungent pyramids of debris
as evidence of existence before a Category 4.

Refuge Chaos

Here we stand
bedraggled beyond recognition or surprise
in line for another free meal
and inevitable emotional checkup
that comes from surviving
sludgy-assed, crusty-eyed disaster.

We no longer hear the children crying
because they've somehow faded
into the auditorium reverb of distress calls
and fever-pitch worry
over what might be crawling under our skin.

My bunkmate refuses to climb 4 feet to the upper bunk
so I do it and pull the pillow over my head
to drown out her toothache moaning
and this incessant wailing of 7000 refugees.

All I want is a Valium and release papers.
Maybe to lay my head on the shoulder
of this Madonna social worker
listening so kindly to my pleas and stories
of a mother waiting with a hot shower
and hotter bowl of sausage gumbo
her daughters will eat no matter how steamy outdoors
or frigid indoors.

I miss my chance
when someone lost and found a baby
and the wheel-chair lady rolls up
with a cup of cookies and swollen ankles.
Three heart attacks and a by-pass
moves her ahead of my bad nerves
and my bunkmate's broken tooth.

Notes From Refuge

Things to do after disaster:

Count cash
Call mother
Smoke cheap cigarettes
Contact FEMA
Stand in line
Drink free coffee
Mingle with refugees
Attend funerals
Eat free food
Contact FEMA
Contact Red Cross
Drive to mother
Visit childhood
Drink home brew beer
Rant
Accept donations
Bake potato bread
Collect memories
Contact FEMA
Write poetry
Write letters
Write notes
Borrow clothes
Bury your lover
Contact FEMA
Get free gloves
Get free masks
Get free shots
Drive to disaster
Sift through rubble
Drag bodies to river
Search for familiar faces
Pray to unknown gods

Detour Of Destiny

One day they'll say a poet flipped this coin,
another detour of destiny in a long line
of fuckups leading to deliberate obscurity.
Wooden objections carry no weight in museum lives,
but should they carry over to sons and boys of war,
freedom of will may break structure placed so
indelicately between stronghold.

Is there no place left where the poet may speak
without fear of the *machina*
we the people placed into
God's and our funded trust?
Being tap-wired into submission will make us
what we fear most and we will die as our own enemy.

They will censor me if I say there is no
democracy in oil rigs and other weapons –
if I say there is no democracy at all
except on parched documents in heavy glass.
Propaganda is propaganda no matter the metaphor or rhyme.
O that Jesus and his daughters would return with a vengeance!
Who could hide from such wrath as a woman cheated
of her birthright?

Tyranny thrives under distant fire and fear of the unknown
makes us all stronger, but not enough to not kill you.
Nothing can hide us from our own soil.
Nor will our souls be saved by paper-tales
hammered out in antique machines of mass destruction.
I long for long-lost purple mountain grit,
honesty among thieves, and gentlefolk side-by-side
defending honor and home.

Ah, but this too is only a tale of hardship and woe . . .
falling somewhere between political comfort and a sinking city.

Tempting Fate

So if rain dare not fall upon the undead,
why did we shake our fists?
And point those damn itchy fingers twice a week or more?
Who gave you the authority to kill my brother?
Or make me ride out this storm
with nothing more than hunger in my belly
and a need to make someone else pay for your neglect?

O yea of little faith, much arrogance, and no bread . . .
Bury your minor regrets and mourn the bloated bodies,
not the loot.
Give the people their due of mold and destruction.
Hiding places are scarce when tanks roll in with tides
and everything you know is toxland waste.

Single Morning

Present tense granted
you are the story that counts.

The dead woman
surfaces from the burning house,
nameless, faceless, with no guise
of perfection or monotony.
She is you or me or her
and all of us in fenced anxiety
of false identity and crises.

What do you inherit from revision?
  A single morning and a plate of rage.

The scorched dream is never rescued
because a refuge will fail
and danger takes its place.
They watch and sing off-key
'hallelujahs' as you eat
from your own stomach
digesting woman from the inside first.

If we know the equation,
the carving scars seal
in our skulls with a motive
too ravenous to explore alone.
So we write archives of potential
and wait for someone to discover
our blood on the floor –
perhaps pull us from the fire.

Signature Hamartia

Here in the common halls of substance,
labyrinth green with serenity and despair
mingled and anti-depressed numb. . .
it seems holocaustic madness is tolerable after all.

This is, after all, my dream.
Illusions I cooked up myself over a weak fire
and a circle of rare stones.
Twisting skeleton keys in academic doors
until the last on the left opened with surreal ease.

But ill-timing, my signature hamartia,
often places me at naturally rebellious front lines,
meandering on frowns of fortune
and downdraft swerves,
scraping elbows and knees in another occasion
to cheat the reaper's fist by a nick
of something more consistent than time.

One never knows when a dream will turn on you.
Take you from ambrosial transcendence
to Category 4 forces of will against yours
in a single rapid eye movement.
Dragging core and psyche to mortal boundaries
only to dump you at Hades gate in a box-truck,
holding a manual scripted in Coptic ideograms
and no compass to navigate home.

I cannot wake from this dream just yet—
because I no longer seep anger on the world
or myself for the lack of synchronicity between us,
and shifting at 46 mph with a drink in your hand,
a poem in your head,
a storm on your back is difficult, even in dreams.

II.

Suicide and Grace Notes

E. Bathory's Prayer

The heavens look down upon me with such fierce disdain.
I am a killer, a murderer of girls whose beauty outlasts mine.

O Goddess, release me from this hell-born vanity,
From the mirror of soulless glass and tinkling auras of red!

I wish I had not killed them.
To let them live instead to see their beauty fade like mine
In this ashen urn like spotted dogs in heat!

Does no one feel remorse for the killer?
Does no one see behind her frozen eyes
A soul? A weeping bitter soul
Entombed in useless, flaccid flesh?

God, can you hear me? I repent for taking their lives.
You may release me from this body.

I am not alive, I am not dead,
I am not myself.
This bliss of enigma, this outrage of torment
Is more than I can bear.

God, can you hear me? Release me from your grasp!
I am the child of the devil instead, and he loves me
In ways you cannot.

Wanting, wanting, wanting
A single word from you,
But you will not turn to me
Because I am a killer.

You have hidden me in a lump of your clay.
Brown and riddled with pebbles of sand,
Irritating this shell of being I am banished into.

How long, O God, how long will you punish me?
I have repented dutifully for their pitiful lives
Over and over again.

If you were an honest God, you would admit
I saved them
From graying hair and sagging breasts
And spots upon their brows!

Can you not forgive sadistic inclinations
Inspired by blood and Black Beg?

These were your holy gifts to me!
Endowed properly in your own mortar-stone shack.
Your own circular logic of graceful redemption.

O God, if you cannot forgive,
Then release me at once
To the mighty forces of darkened wind!

Lift me to the edge of my Hades!
Drop me into insanity again, for there, I know myself.
There, I am home.

Prière d'E. Báthory

French translation by Richard Turek

Les cieux me regardent avec un si féroce dédain.
Je suis une meurtrière, tueuse de filles dont la beauté m'eût survécu

Ô déesse, délivre-moi de cette vanité née de l'enfer
Du miroir au verre sans âme et aux éclatantes auras de rouge!

Je regrette de les avoir tuées.
J'aurais pu les laisser vivre et voir leur beauté comme la mienne
Faner
Dans cette urne cendrée comme des chiennes en chaleurs!

Personne n'éprouve-t-il donc de remords pour l'assassin?
Personne ne peut-il voir derrière ses yeux glacés
Une âme ? Une âme amère en pleurs
Emmurée dans une enveloppe de chair flasque et inutile?

Dieu, m'entends-tu? Je me repens d'avoir pris leur vies.
Tu peux me délivrer de ce corps.

Je ne suis ni vivante, ni morte,
Je ne suis pas moi-même.
Cette félicité du mystère, cet outrage du tourment
C'est plus que je n'en puis supporter.

Dieu, m'entends-tu ? Délivre-moi de ton étreinte!
Car je suis la fille du démon, et lui m'aime
De façons que tu ne pourras jamais.

Je veux, J'attends, J'espère
Un simple mot de toi,
Mais tu t'es détourné de moi
Parce que je suis une meurtrière.

Tu m'a dissimulé dans un morceau de ton argile.
Brune et énigmatique avec des grains de sable,
Irritant cette coquille d'être dans laquelle j'ai été bannie.

Combien, combien de temps encore ô dieu vas-tu me punir?
Je me suis tant repentie pour leur misérables vies
Encore, et encore.

Si tu étais un Dieu honnête, tu admettrais
Que je n'ai fait que les sauver.
Des cheveux gris, des poitrines flêtries
Et des taches sur leur fronts!

Ne peux-tu pardonner des penchants sadiques
Inspirés par le sang et les Noires Prières?

Ceux-ci furent pourtant tes saints présents pour moi!
Dûment établies dans ta demeure de pierre et de mortier.
Ta propre logique absurde de grâcieuse rédemption.

O Dieu, si tu ne peux pardonner,
Alors livre-moi tout de suite
Aux puissantes forces du vent obscur!

Hisse-moi au bord de mon Hadès!
Précipite-moi à nouveau dans la folie, car là-bas, je sais qui je suis
Là-bas, je suis chez moi.

Suicide Notes

You look dead in my eyes
And I am amused at the psychoanalyst mask
Falling over your face as you reproach me again
For my carelessness,
My inability to write suicide notes.
It's my own fault, you say, for placing myself here
Under rigid rule semblances of mordant life.

In a battered city of purple bruises and buckled streets,
You're lucky to find one memory . . .
One poem to sum up your life.

Pick up the damn pen and write your death,
You say in a stern voice.
Grow some balls, find words to die by.
Surely you have an apology
For the mother who'll find the note.
For sisters who'll sleep in your unmade bed,
Friends who'll miss work to attend your cowardice.
Surely you'll compensate them with a word or two
In letters they'll bury in mahogany boxes.

I'll never understand, of course, how to do this.
Or why the apologies for death will not come.
Snippets of image flood my consciousness,
Unwelcome rays of hope when all I want
Is to swallow a red bottle and witness fluidity in clouds.

Losing My Balance While Rising

After Johannes Vermeer's "Woman Holding a Balance"

Seeking a way in or out
He watches me rise
He looks for serenity in my devotions
Blank words offered as though he knows
The suffering of losing one's self

I will create another
Shape a new mask to cover inherent fear
And shed translucid beams in marvelous imitation

My hand steadies the balance
Over belly swollen with something
I do not know

I will weigh and wait
For this outcome
Circle bead between thumb and finger
While rising above all misery of contemplation

Bipolar Rage

Of all the props we might have carried toward this end,
I never thought to include broken windows,
four of your naked friends, and a small pair of scissors.
Even through your drunken rages and bipolar moods
I did not prepare for this,
nor did I expect to miss you later.
I drive your old neighborhood
and they wave at me.

I have no use for what they offer.

I admit exploring your world
sets me apart from everyone here.
Now I have butterfly scars and a reason to die
peacefully in my sleep while you watch
waves lick my swollen body.
I want to believe it's only lack of familiarity
that scares me now, but I know it's you.
If I weren't bleeding and desperate, I'd gather up
these chunks of flesh again
to lay them at your feet.
Maybe then, I'd understand the fascination
with the grotesque beauty of my own blood,
and the pale blue shadow of yours.

Alter: ego

These are the thoughts I try not to think
the life I'm not leading
but don't bother extending your hand
I'll save myself

It won't be the first time
I pulled out of a grave

You are my tourniquet
and I let you live another day
to abuse all things that matter to you
and I, well . . . you know I mean well

The crimson chaos on the floor
that morning never was and never will be
what we expected

She's gone
the one thing that could've saved you
is gone

So don't look to me for answers
no one gives a damn
and there are none that will sate your need
for more, more, just one more
20 dollar bill oughtta do it

You are my Genie
and I let you sleep another night
in empty bottles, and I, well . . .
meant to wake you, but something always came up

Who the hell cares about what you want anyway
you're just a suicide note away
from a broke-down paradise

Did you really expect me to live
on a razor blade with intact sanity
and your hand cuffed around my ankle

You are the phrase
I coined all those years ago
when I still cared about you and
knew what was holding me here
and I, well . . . I'm sure it meant something
to one of us, but now it's only a puny gesture
to hold your hand that way

These are the thoughts I try not to think
the life I'm not leading
and if you try to save me this time
I, well . . .
will untie this tourniquet
watch you drown in your bottle of blood
and never blink

You are the monster
knocking at my door and I let you
live another night to call me out
at four o' clock in the morning

Where the hell have you been and why
are you holding a silver light on my sins

Breaking Down Divorce

It's such bitter irony that I've ended up here,
having traveled 200 miles with no one to talk to
but me, and you
still can't be shaken.

There's an empty Tequila bottle in the parking lot,
and I think I want to be dead now,
but maybe I just need some sleep.

This thin-walled motel makes me witness
to the man upstairs
preaching gospel
according to the savior in that bottle.

His woman must be on her knees by now,
repenting in sticky breaths
that could be bare feet sinking in and out of mud.

We are both just soulless survivors, she and I.
Looking for clipped salvation in distance,
or a religious drunk.

She must know the rules of marriage.
I do.
But when the levee breaks,
we toss them away,
stretching just a little dignity
while we wait for the storm's eye,
or the next exit to Eden.

Event Horizon

she falls from madness
with such grace

cadillac manicures
over another glass of wine

she moves in primal rhythm
on the edge of another history lesson
a bird's eye view
of her paper retreat

gemini wizard
housed in glass
peels labels from a deck of cards
tries not to talk
into the mirror

so what if she believes infinity is a number
or event horizons sometimes lie

what's not to love about freedom
and the unborn story of transformation

Ode To H.D.

I dreamed of the wind in your face
it smelled of anemones and olives –
its bitter sting like jelly-fish

Zeus himself roused from sleep
to watch it bear down upon you
he gave it a voice and called it 'woman'

the heat and utter stench stretched
in boredom and sang of your body:
an ill-omened guise of protection

a white star moved across the sky
in harmony with the spirit
yet the flawed tradition flowered

that's the trouble with art, you said
there is enough beauty
and no one to appreciate the dots and dashes

Grace Note One

can you forget the smell of us
naked and spooned after the rainstorm

there in the gravel of Bob's Lawn
and Garden . . .

the burn on my skirt
worth every pound of regret
you felt for her

it wasn't enough to keep you
from lunch and later
your hands on the couch

the thing with the panties was brilliant
how long before your breath slowed to normal

an erotic rush of elevator
we knew she was near-by
I think she was your wife by then
but I can't be sure I was lost
somewhere between the rise
and fall of the third or fourth
floor and you were still
only working on the novel
idea of one woman at a time

Blue Skies

for my Pablo

With you it's always blue skies, palomino ponies.
And when you walked down from Mount Sinai,
with your face on fire,
an apparition of a lighthouse witness,
I knew I loved you.

But this twilight is gone,
and your soul clenched in mine
still casts sad nets.

Heaven knows I want to compare
the ocean to your eyes, here.

Instead, I cast you in light
of mortal flames and hide
my trembling hands
so you can't touch them.
Your perfection never wore well on me.
I'm only the rough peasant
body of a woman.

Still, the memory of you emerges from the night around me.
I am deserted like the wharves at dawn.

How cruel of you to give me this poem.
To salt my wound with reminders
of what you have with her –
a small flock of tundra swans,
and morning kisses in bed.

Maja's Seduction

She came fully clothed.
Laced hands shadow her breasts,
she unfolds in elegant pose.
As Goya lifts his reflection,
his eyes rest on Maja's ripe peaches,
dipped in cream.
He wonders if her nipples are pink,
maybe brown.
If her belly is soft,
legs long enough
to add symmetry
when slightly bent
     or open.
With slow strokes,
he undresses her,
breathing deep
the scent
that becomes his muse.

Your Hands

On this
the occasion of reunion
this grand fugue of communal love
I love that you know me well enough to know
I hide in closets with notebook and pen
recording everything
    like your hands . . .
conducting this beautiful conversation

    your hands . . .
stroking my hair
my cheek
a master score of scarlet fever

your hands . . .
a symphony of grace notes along my spine
melodic fluidity of laughter
awakening my muse
arousing curiosity over why
we circled above each other so long
only to land at the same time in this same place
with me watching your hands

Grace Note Two

there you are again in perfect sulk
your arms waving in drama-flair scenario
as though an audience of thousands were watching
and feeling, really feeling your distress

ah, here comes the flip of your ink-dipped ringlet
over a graceful shoulder
each movement gazelle-like and over-extended
driving your point of rejection outward

you are art in precise tilts of your wrist
beautiful grace with Baryshnikov thighs
painted black and simultaneously innocent

the constant questioning of your sanity
drives you insane, yet you move forward
without it and play martyr to perfection
your body language of graffiti and poetry
angle in lines only you understand

there is no telling what you will say next
or what draws the ladies to your gypsy-esque charm
so you prepare for it all with dewy lashes
and elegantly poised hips
one hand shading your notably green eyes
the other lingering limply on my thigh
just in case
no one else is watching

I Want

coins from camelot jackpot
a flu shot
and cool shoes
voodoo shiraz
jack-hammer-jazz
and drive-by-blues

eyes of jezebel bombshell
ankle-bells
sherbert-flirts
blackberry-breath
cashmere-death
and wind-swept skirts

poems in project dialect
indirect
ruby-lipped
juggalo-thugs
spark-plug drugs
and clock-out script

Moon Stroke

Even from here I knew
you were laughing
tonight at 11:11
because I suddenly could not stop
what began in small chuckles
by a Bridget Jones-like spark
then a magic mushroom cloud
primal laugh as good as a cry

My mind's eye saw your face
laughing with me the way we always do
after a stroke of moon
in perfect circles
and undisturbed semantics
of Eve-leaves
and apples from another realm

Tattoo

The 13th angel gets fairy wings
and fat red curls that never get brushed.

She's smaller than the others,
sits on the stem of a blue flower:
   infinity in three stars.

The angel on her left is faded
and her favorite contemplation.
Mystery with no resolution
and better that way.

He is a boy who choked
on a seed of his pride,
found love in the eclipse
of a rusty comet
with a girl who smells heather.

A hologram lover in dark stains,
speaks to dreamers on Sunday morning
and likes the sound of his voice.

The 13th angel gets a name like *Faith*
and laughs at the irony.
She can't control what she sees
through the artist's crooked eye.

The Wreck Revisited

now that the wreck is uncovered
i'll take you as my Cousteau

the flippers aren't as awkward now
and the black rubber has faded
into my skin like a rash

there was never a need for chisels
a knife will do

nothing was set in stone . . .
only paper. The book is water-logged
and the ladder still hangs

but there is nothing innocent about it

a black-widow spider
lingers where it should not
on the word maps that hang
between coral reefs and other dead things

i have the courage to go back to this scene
to write my name beside yours
because it is my drowned face
that slept with open eyes

i was not left to rot
because you rescued me
from the silent circles
of power and indifference

Things Mina Loy Couldn't Say

I.

Get out of my way.
You and your nine inch identity
don't know who you're dealing with.
I've made grown men cry
by the edge of my tongue.
Made them come
to my understanding
of his mental masturbation
in seismic orgasms.

II.

Woman, you're a fool.
A mere fragment of a whole
cumulation of falsehoods.
Defined in black and white absurdity—
a caricature in silhouette.
But the wrench from the page
is too much for your delicate constitution.
You conserve your energy for desire
to be loved by that which does not.

III.

O sacred Virgin!
How dare you stare at me
with glassy eyes of complacency?
Strike your damn bargain
on someone else's street.
Your exchange of flesh
goes against laws of reciprocity.
You receive nothing
but a skin-sack of potential perpetuation.

Nagasaki Butterfly

Cio-Cio-San just committed suicide again.
In milk-honey anguish,
she ripped her belly open to honor
the memory of dead fathers.

She carefully misplaced her son
in a world strange,
intolerable to butterflies
or angels with one black wing.
His face was sunset over Zenkoji Temple,
a heel stone of Neolithic piscinas,
everything she knew about a faceless God and mercy.

His name is Trouble,
and he refuses my hand.
He hears my words,
but cannot understand that he can touch me,
that his eyes are like raisins and Cio-Cio-San is dead today.

III.

Fragments of Chaos Suspended From the Whole

The Other Side

So here it ends . . . another opportunity to bridge the gap of a centuries old war. Mina Loy said it best . . . we are to blame for our own subjugation . . . it was the division between our sisters and our selves that kept us from reforming legislation, but even worse . . . from revising the myths of the feminine as a lesser being . . . wives, witches, or whores – those were the choices given to us and still we stand here today . . . divided by petty temper tantrums and an unwillingness to forgive . . .

So if I say no one can harm me . . . and believe it to be truth, then what should I fear? And if my reality resists all boundaries, who can stop me from myself? Am I a slave to the excruciating rhythms of gravity and time? Or just a passerby in a field of something like a dream, but fluid and warm to the touch?

When you were a girl with pink ponytails and a freckled back, did you cut off the tails of lizards and giggle while they squirmed? Did they beg you to stop through beads of eyes burning with pain and fear of the unknown?

Was there ever a time when you, queen of despair, saw another woman and didn't feel threatened by the fact that she is closer to your goal than you?

There is no war to speak of, except in the minds of the wounded soldiers, breathing heavy in their corsets and bonnets stuffed with shame . . . dressed for a night ride, but silenced by their past . . . limping along like one-winged faeries in a glass bowl . . .
This is your life on the other side of that door . . .

Kitchen Poetics

My daughter and mother know
the art of stirring stovetop summations.
I blend words into the mix and watch my mother
plump, red-faced excited.

She remembers the soup kitchen in '39 or '40
and the extra serving of bread once.
A surplus of butter in '41 went to the school children
in hard blocks.

My daughter rolls her tongue along the spoon,
adds a dash of salt.
She'll add a handful of peppered words about dignity next.

I'll grab my canvas, or maybe the camera,
because I won't want to forget this.
Mom moves toward the oven and a story
about the New Orleans neighbor who stole twenty dollars.

A fresh-from-the-country woman
taken by big city toughs.
She clicks her tongue and laughs
at the near escape from stairwell hoodlums in '56.

My daughter never looks up from the potatoes
she's pounding into dry flakes for bread.
She doesn't want to join a girls club of spandex
and awkward propositions.

The opportunity to disagree with both doesn't come often,
so I write the note to excuse her.

The afternoon simmers with stories of '68
and small wonders of survival a year later.
Mom stirs the air with tomato sauce and memories
poised between atonement and pride.

My daughter lifts her head, finally, she hears and smells
heritage wrapped in a neat paradigm.
My mother folds flour and egg into my daughter's bowl,
I add melted cheese.

Lousiana Garden In August

for Tommy

The scorch of July weighs heavy
on eight green tomatoes in an August garden.
Black spot and long-legged insects work round the clock.
We've long abandoned them
for books and mechanical air –
both relentless in intrigue and coquetry.
Tommy and I share orange popsicles
on the couch of blue jean dreams,
swapping mind chatter stories of heroes and outlaws.

The garden was splendid last year.
Buckets of invitation and promise.
But with all these dark castles to build,
teeth to pull, and knees to scrub,
Earth must care for itself today.

The wooden stakes are chipped and grey now,
leaning heavily away from afternoon sun.
Flecks of fresh mold,
scattered on my crumbling leaves,
like some accidental artwork,
match the toy soldiers
carelessly left there all summer,
fighting a fanciful battle
handed down from Tommy's sovereign hand.

We stand back to admire the disaster of our garden.
Once, we braved Louisiana's claustrophobic heat,
dug our fingers in its black roux soil.

We have eight green tomatoes in an August garden.

Precipice Of a Third Story Edge

brown spots, brown spots
brown spots everywhere

brown spots on my face—
the one thing inherited from my father

brown spots on the dog
licking the brown spots on my face
inherited from my father

brown spots on my skirt
coffee spilled
while the brown-spot dog licked my face

brown spots on my car
pigeons
living in my brown-spot tree

brown spots on my psyche—
a father who gave me nothing
but brown spots

brown spots
on the ceiling
of my survival house

brown spots
on my lungs
and cigarettes

brown spots
on my sister's blue eyes

brown spots
below the third-story edge
where someone before me jumped

A Fragment Of Chaos Suspended From The Whole

so it all comes down to circles and squares
deciphered from an aerial position
a bridge of word and number can too easily implode

but this is my own chaos
it contains nothing
of importance like yours

someone in a mirror once said
the carrier must be a woman
look for her under a dogwood

at 3:10 or 11 a.m. it will come to you
that you remember only two lines
of the poem you were going to write
and sometimes the rain sounds
like a voyeur at your bedroom window

if azaleas are blooming today
you might find the courage
to nod at the man with black shoes
or remind someone to breathe

this day will last a lifetime
in a dream of euphoria
and moonlight sex
appeals to the masses
engrossed in the thing itself

if the road of eyes
corrodes the living then dead
community purpose
unravels in a brainstorm
of something like love
but liquid

Surviving Identity

I thought I would always hate you,
and when you died I knew
I could never love you.
The difference became my center
in a series of quarter moons
and sad-eyed poems I did not write.
It was always you standing at the door,
waving a bag full of yourself and
a promise already broken.

The villagers were scared of you
but hid the secret in the palm of your hand.
It was me you made a model of
from clay and dark wood.
You left it exposed,
never expecting rot.

This is my confession:
I am you, father.
Your roots finally took hold somewhere in my feet.
I, too, can make my exit graceful
and bury my head in sand or an oven
to scale blood-stained walls,
and finally understand the hunger of obsession
in surviving identity.

Three Photographs, Three Days

for Keith (1954-2005)

Now that you are dead,
and I have spent the last 3 days
reliving the madness that was our lives,
I know salvation forged from refuge.

The self-induced illusion of mirrors
lining the house we created of stones
and sticks of dynamite,
has finally crumbled.

The ashes of your life
and body drift in circles
outnumbered by squares and disbelievers.

How comfortable you must be now
in your default redemption and weightlessness.

Here we were, my love—
on the streets of plated gold,
borrowing a minute and escaping yet another
tragedy by the skin of our collective dentistry.
Skimming the surface of a water-color dream
in multi-dimensional confusion.

You are now my Patron Saint of Saturday night,
and I know that you will keep it flowing,
like the flooded trail of drama and intrigue
we called a marriage for the sake of others
who couldn't see us drowning in rivers
of glass and amber-stained reality.

I rummaged through our secrets today
without stopping to think
and you were there in my delusion.
Wishing me well while reminding me
of my presence in your death
by my absence in your life.

So how does it feel now to know
those mysterious sounds that haunted me?
Our own blood beating in measures
we couldn't stop counting,
yet we never heard the rhythms
bouncing back and forth and back again.

I have only 3 photographs of you now.
A sad progression of the life we loved and lost
in purple haze misery and interdependent allowances
of mischief and mayhem.

I would have shed my own skin to save yours, luv.
But pride got the best of pride
and we burned out, wasting another chance
to untangle the mysterious bravado that motivated me
and terrified you all those years ago.

There is small salvation in memories and photographs
of a life misused now that you are dead,
and I have spent the last 3 days
reliving the madness that was our lives.

Reflection Of Fear

it's always the last note
that magnifies
   suspends in emptiness
unripe thoughts
we don't dare think
   that avalanche like young snow

we hear loudest
   the pauses
syncopate   the next beat
rhythm held moments away
from the sharpest edge
      sex
one   static   moment
before the rush
of immortality

nothing breathes

  except the moment

a familiar beat
   almost alive

the fade of passing cars
rise of air
   at the tunnel's exit
shadows swimming
over a moonlit lake
      as soundless as melting ice
wildfired forests

it's always nights
   unwarped by sleep
that we try to remember

where the heart is hidden
   how water holds
the body afloat
when to breathe
        if it lets you fall . . .

Near-Drowning

This wasn't a murmuring waterfall,
but some lingering memory of my birth.

Alluvial shell with webbed hands,
before water burst over my body
and I became whole.

The end of passage is never clear in a drowning.
Throat and lungs burn,
gallons of blood pound in the head,
eyes bulge in blue-black circles.

But surfacing brings visions of clarity.
Stains of memory,
constructed undefined.
Drowning comes easy.
A complacent fall into negation.

But the body always wants
one last pull of air.

Teacups and Tin Men

All afternoon we move in and out of summer shadow.
Intricate gestures of tragedy scored blindly.
The neighbor boy plays music to die by for six long hours.
Sad melodies that remind us of you.

Bells, bells, bells of cathedrals embrace us
like old lovers in old movies.

Ravens flicker past your holy field of white perennials,
and I believe I can hear you
over the impasse of division on solid ground.

But upon closer inspection,
my own mind speaks
memories of fever-fed madness in dull gray.
Our mindful worries and argument
over teacups and tin men,
swamp-life acrylics and vase-flower poetry.

As engine noises and black-shade hazards
float easily over this summer scene now,
I am reminded why
the life we are brought back to
costs more than before
the bother of existence became habit.

Earth/Air

for Theresa

I.
I don't know where to find my mother today. She's out catching Jupiter drops while writing words in a sunbeam journal. She serves rainbows for dinner while her eyes reflect cloud memories. She has too much heart they say, but those damn winged feet always get her from drama to intrigue without consequence. She'll never learn to play in the sand like I did. She's always chasing winged things and smiles when she says, "It only counts if the wind blows toward you." I must be the only girl whose mother speaks in poetry and sees ambiguity in everything. A mother with a helium balloon where the heart should be. I would love to visit her, but she won't dare settle into dust or let mud touch her feet when the moon passes Sagittarius and Orion is polishing his belt.

II.
I must sweep the edges of my daughter tonight, but the air is so pure on Venus. I wish just once she could see the moon from here and understand that earth tones really do look beautiful on her. She is an untended garden. Wreathing flowers for hours in her hair. A wood-nymph whistling birdsongs to beckon elves and fairy godmothers. If I must be grounded, she's the best company for it. She doesn't sneeze when the wind kicks up. She eats the rainbows I serve for dinner and waves politely at my Mercurial gravitation. A mud-wrap spa is what I'll give for her birthday. She has too many moonstones buried in those sienna clay pots. And twice already today, I've seen her sifting sand from her fingers, wishing it would rain.

Primal

although she was
a woman of words
she could find none
to fit her reason

Insanity they said

premenstrual

postpartum

   menopause

cliches

to excuse bad behavior
she needed a word

that explained
tender breasts

blood-stained sheets

giving birth
from the sin of your sweat

dead things
in the box under your bed

why it feels damned
good to scream
in the car when no one can hear

Theresa's Rant

she wants to look like Britney Spears
has no idea she does

she's drunk on depression today
summer curved and bikini-pink
she wants to airbrush perfect thighs
and work machines all day

her career's gone with the storm so
body images and tomorrow
are themes of today
this is no time for poetics
so we rant over home-brew
and too many cigarettes

*finding out who you are should be a paying gig
because it's enough to handle on its own*

*who the hell is spinning this wheel
and when is it gonna turn our way*

*let's just cuddle with kittens
and live in a giant house
or a castle run by dogs*

she thinks it's weird she used to play
with dogs and imaginary friends
and for two years had neither

she's going to dream something big one day
and accept it with little grace
save the world for herself and from herself
by laying out stones on tarot
fairy-winged in bookstores

nose-thumbing mundane critics
who don't know what they believe
or why

what else does the man want
spirituality is something you do in small circles
church is for the masses

her screenplay is in limbo
because she can't make the characters real
or hard enough for her own taste
Candy in the mall and Jewels will really
fuck up your mind

the sequel will make money
if she can learn to download . . .
computers can be so confusing:
sometimes the whole CD plays
when you only want to hear track 2

vampire flicks and books are interesting
but overdone so she interviews toys
bums cigarettes
because daddy fired her last week

Jesus Christ, things are complicated for martyrs

women who kill men get a death sentence
and men who kill women never get caught
unless the body decays
I'm killing myself over loneliness
drowning in my beer
and you never even notice me
sitting in the back drop
I see all

I know nothing
dying to be seen
for just one moment
look at me
while the blood spills on the floor

Voodoo Moss

There's a naked eye moon
For these painless suicide poems
If we search for Lucifer's halo
In Baba Yaga's dream
We might find a night child
Even in this fading light

There's a Sundance for Echidne
In fields of ripe pomegranates
But you're sleepwalking
Through someone else's life
And carelessly misplace the invitation

There's a black crucifix on Babylon Dragons
And descendants of Cain
Will pepper your beauty
Drink your wine-stained intent
And bury seeds of your thought

Raven-winged mystery
And fork-tongue lies will not stop
Stone temple demons
From whispering your ear

May rustic angels and Jesus
Loom forever above your small bloody scars

To commemorate the night
We will paint Voodoo Moss dolls
In red-hair controversy
Let us carve ancient scrolls
Of willow wand witches

Let us follow a dance of Baron Samedi
In slow marching rhythms
Just in time for your long-awaited death

End Note

To construct my death to your liking,
I'll first find a sharp edge.
Thin, serrated armor, like your tongue.
Drag it across my words in mindful precision.
Create a defining moment of non-existence,
Inking pages in blood,
Dropping stones in my pocket.

Because you look dead in my eyes,
I surrender
Without consent . . .
To write these bloody notes
No one will read
Until I am dead.

About the Author

Lana Maht Wiggins returned to New Orleans, her mother's native city, in the summer of 2005 to begin a teaching career at the University of New Orleans. During this time, she began collecting stories and experiences of her beloved NOLA until the storm of the century blew through on August 29, 2005 and changed her entire world and the focus of this book. While seeking refuge from a ravaged and broken New Orleans, Lana drew upon her personal experiences of disaster to create these poignant nouveau-narrative poems of life in limbo as a refugee. Lana creates a multitude of voices and visions in these poems meant as poetic portraits of women who have lost everything, including hope, love, identity, voice, and life.

Lana's poetry has captured an international audience of readers, and she has been initiated into the International Writer's Group, *Encres de Sang*, where she was the guest poet/lecturer in Paris, France at the 3rd annual International Gathering of Writers in May 2008. Lana Maht Wiggins has been published in "The Southwestern Review," "Poems for a Livable Planet," "The Deep South Writer's Chapbook," "Dance to Death," "Words-Myth," "Moondance," "Knock," and "The Smoking Poet."

Currently, Lana resides in Lafayette, Louisiana where she is an Instructor of English at the University of Louisiana. Lana Maht Wiggins earned her Master of Arts degree in Creative Writing in 2001 from the University of Louisiana, Lafayette. Lana received the Judge Felix Voorhies Award for Creative Writing and a Jon Z. Bennet Award in The Deep South Writer's Conference Poetry Contest in 1996 and was a finalist in the 2006 Marsh Hawk Poetry Contest. *Notes from Refuge* is Lana's first full-length collection of poems.

Photo © 2008, Lauren Doré, Rock This Life Photography

www.ingramcontent.com/pod-product-compliance
Lightning Source LLC
Chambersburg PA
CBHW071026080526
44587CB00015B/2514